INDUSTRIAL LOCOMOTIVES & IN

1: NORTH EAST ENGLA

Copyright Book Law Publications 2010
ISBN 978-1-907094-91-0

INTRODUCTION

This album is a compilation of images from the collection of Neville Stead. The subjects cover a broad swathe of industrial locomotive types, along with illustrations of the many installations where they worked or were serviced and stabled. For various reasons, not least it is the favourite industrial area of the compiler, the north-east of England was the choice of this, the first such album in this series.

Besides the obvious coal mining related pictures, there are those covering quarrying, ship building, steel making and dockside scenes.

Helping out with the captions, Dave Holroyde must also be acknowledged for thoroughly reading through the final proofs and bringing his vast knowledge of all things 'Industrial' to bear on the manuscript. Neville Stead also read through the proofs and added much of interest.

(*previous page*) **NCB Hartley Main No.20 at Seaton Delaval, 29th March 1953. This former Glasgow & South Western Rly. No.171, was sold by the LMS (No.17196) in 1926 and was then used to run trains from Kirkheaton Colliery to the LNER exchange sidings at Darras Hall. It was No.1 in the Kirkheaton Col. Co. Ltd. fleet of one! When the colliery closed in 1930, this engine was apparently left in the shed there, neglected and moribund. In 1942, to help the Allied war effort it was overhauled prior to taking up employment with the Board of Trade, Mines Department at Cambois opencast, numbered MD425. In 1946 it transferred to Backworth then, some three years later in October 1949, it was given a further lease of life and moved to Seaton Delaval. It was scrapped in April 1953. The original G&SWR class numbered some eighteen locomotives designed by Manson and built between 1897 and 1899. All entered service on the LMS but withdrawals began in 1925 and the last one had gone by 1933. The class was an updated version, with all-over cabs, of the eighty-odd 0-6-0s introduced by Smellie in the ten year period from 1881.** *NES 8539.*

Printed and bound by The Amadeus Press, Cleckheaton, West Yorkshire
First published in the United Kingdom by Book Law Publications, 382 Carlton Hill, Nottingham, NG4 1JA

Seaton Delaval Colliery - 4th September 1953. One of the oldest collieries in this part of Northumberland, Seaton Delaval is recorded as lifting its first coal in 1841 and the timber-built headgear on the right was probably associated with that first production. Latterly, or at least since the 1930s, coal has been brought to the surface via the steel girder headgear on the left although the headgear is 'new' - circa 1930 - the shaft over which it was built also dated from the nineteenth century. Note the likeness of the two original winding houses, with a third one silhouetted by the two spoil heaps overlooking the mine. The profile of the winding houses, along with their outward appearance, bring medieval siege towers to mind! This pit employed around 800 men at the time of this photographic record but none seem to be about the place just now. Nor do there appear to be any locomotives, just lots of wooden bodied NCB internal user wagons. At Vesting Day, Seaton Delaval was producing in excess of a quarter of a million tons of saleable coal per annum, a reasonable amount by any measure considering the relatively small number of miners. However, during the fifties' a slow decline set in and by 1955 the output was down to about 180,000 tons a year. Note the large stack of wooden pit props in the yard, a measure that underground mechanisation had not yet reached this place. It is unlikely that it ever did because in 1960 the colliery closed, its reserves apparently exhausted. The location of this pit, in the southern part of Northumberland, positioned it at the centre of one of the most intensely mined areas of Britain, the next pit to the north being just a mile away, that to the west a mile away, etc., etc. It was certainly a coal rich district with numerous seams, which kept tens of thousands of souls employed for over 150 years. *NES 8534.*

The locomotive sheds at Seaton Delaval, 4th September 1953. Obviously some major maintenance was carried out here, the massive shearlegs at the side of the shed being a serious piece of kit by any measure. Note the similarity between colliery headframes and this lifting tackle - coincidence or was that the way the local engineers built anything with girders? Four locomotives are in view, two unidentified Robert Stephenson & Hawthorn outside cylinder 0-6-0 saddle tank engines with full National Coal Board insignia stand facing the shed, whilst the shearlegs road stables an 0-6-0 tender engine numbered 3 with N.C.B. initials on the tender. The 0-6-0T on the right is Hartley Main No.29., again the abbreviated N.C.B. adorns the side tank. The rolling stock is another mixture typical of these industrial installations. The open wagon is self explanatory whilst the three vans could be used for anything from gunpowder to tool vans although none of them appear to have seen recent employment. The timber reclamation pile/area is yet another phenomenon of industry - save it because it might come in handy one day! *NES 8535.*

Cambois Colliery No.11 is just about to set back on to another train of loaded hoppers prior to making a trip to the staiths at North Blyth. The course of its coming two mile journey took it south along the coastline, passing nothing but low profile sand dunes, bordering the North Sea, with very little, if any, shelter from the prevailing easterly winds. In winter the winds sometimes had a very low chill factor and engine crews required some form of protection from possible exposure not to mention utter discomfort. This former Southern Railway 'E1' tank, once numbered No.2143 and with London, Brighton & South Coast origins back to 1879, had been adapted to give some kind of protection by infilling the doorway of the cab on either side of the entrance. Added to that is a drop-down, now rolled-up, waterproof sheet which appears now to be in the summertime position. Purchased by the Cowpen Coal Co. in 1931, the 0-6-0T seems dwarfed by the hopper wagon to which is was ready to be attached. It would be interesting to know just how many of these wagons the engine could haul along the near level route. Getting the wagons onto the staiths however was another matter and no doubt another engine was employed to propel the wagons, a few at a time, up the steep inclines to the elevated staith. Just when this engine was purchased by the colliery company is not known neither is the date when it was withdrawn, or its fate thereafter. The colliery from which it was working, Cambois, raised its first coal in the 1860s and was winding up to 400,000 tons of coal each year for much of its NCB existence. Like many of the coastal mines in the north-east of England, a lot of its take came from seams beneath the sea although by 1968 it was worked out and abandoned. *NES 8527.* 5

Cambois No.11 in its National Coal Board guise as No.11B, condemned and awaiting scrapping at an unknown date. Besides the different legends adorning the tank and bunker sides, the engine has undergone a few more changes over the intervening years since the previous photograph was taken. The air tank has been removed from its position beneath the bunker. Some of the pipework around the boiler has also gone but note the strengthening fillets attached to each bufferbeam by rivets. Obviously fifty-odd years working for the main line railways did not prepare it for the twenty or so years working in industry. *NES 8527A.*

No.36, a USA 0-6-0 tank (Davenport , Iowa No.2595 of 1944). USATC 6006. To Hartley Main Colliery, Seaton Delaval, May 1947. Scrapped Killingworth October 1953. Photographed 18th October 1953, at Hartley Main shortly before its final journey. Only having been employed by the NCB for six years or so, it makes you wonder what catastrophe befell this normally reliable design but apparently the NCB could not get spares (it makes you wonder how the Southern Region managed). *NES 8545.*

NCB No.42 at Seaton Delaval, 4th September 1953. RSH 7766 of 1953. The 'Stubby Hawthorn' - Robert Stephenson & Hawthorn's own design' albeit with outside cylinders, to rival the J94 'Austerity' type from Hunslet. Note the legend on the cabside below the engine number states: No.2 AREA. NTH (N&C) DIV. It is yet another permutation of ownership applied to the NCB locomotive fleet which interprets as No.2 Area, Northern (Northumberland & Cumberland) Division. However, the new engine looks somewhat splendid in its lined livery. *NES 8548*.

Ashington NCB passenger station - 1967. This rather austere facility was one of four such stations/halts (Ellington, Linton and North Moor being the other three) situated around the 20-mile long private railway system which served the collieries in the area which could be termed the 'Ashington Triangle' until 1964. Although not easily discernible in this view, both platforms had run-round facilities via the centre road. The coaches employed were all ex-main line vehicles purchased by the NCB and its predecessors and as can be appreciated were rather ancient but nevertheless adequate for the purpose. The nearer rake of coaches contains one ex-Furness Railway vehicle whilst the toplight on the right platform road was one of two former North Eastern carriages allocated to the Ashington fleet (an ex-NER bogie coach from this set is now fully restored and operating on the Tanfield Railway). Being a passenger carrying system, albeit non-paying and private, the Ashington Group railway required Board-of-Trade inspection and, of course, a signalling system. Two examples of the lower quadrant type are in picture whilst just behind the photographer were upper quadrant types too. Note the water tank on the right, a typical colliery installation utilising worn-out Lancashire boilers placed on purpose built brick plinths and good for another twenty years or more. The high ground to the right of the picture was a levelled-out waste tip eventually used for siding accommodation containing full coal wagons, mainly hoppers in this view, of both BR and NCB origin. *NES 8551.*

9

An interesting view of a miners train en route between the collieries of the Ashington group at an unknown date. The motive power is a 'Stubby Hawthorn' with no identification on its front face. The train consists of three coaches, the middle vehicle of which has a door wide open whilst passengers in the first coach peer out at the photographer. Located somewhere near Linton Colliery, the track appears to be somewhat bumpy compared with normal passenger carrying railways but this was, in effect, a private line. The trackbed seems to be made up of pit waste rather than stone ballast but if it did the job - so what. Modellers of mining lines - be aware of the colours of the trackbeds. *NES 8552.*

Ashington locomotive shed, 10th June 1967. The Ashington Coal Company used to have a locomotive fleet which was somewhat varied, not to mention interesting too. The word 'standard' would be hard to apply. However, by 1967 and some years beforehand, the NCB had tried to bring an element of standardisation to the substantial stud of engines. On display here are a number of 0-6-0 saddletanks, both inside and outside cylinders types. Their build dates ranged from 1939 Peckett's to 1956 built Robert Stephenson & Hawthorn's along with a couple of Vulcan Foundry inside cylinder 'Austerities' from 1945. Eventually, over the next five years all the steam motive power used on the Ashington system was replaced by second-hand diesel hydraulic and diesel electric locomotives purchased from British Railways. They survived long enough to see the closure of many collieries in Northumberland and then the return of privatisation to what was left of the industry. Note the well ventilated running shed holding centre stage. To the left of that and slightly behind is the workshop where overhauls of all kinds were performed. During the 1960s a local scrap merchant - W.Willoughby - used part of the NCB property at Ashington to carry out his business which included taking in scrap motor vehicles, redundant machinery of all shapes and sizes but more importantly condemned NCB locomotives from collieries all over the north-east. *NES 8559.*

An undated, though fairly early Fifties view of a couple of the Ashington locomotive fleet in the shed yard. No.13 was a typical industrial side tank with outside cylinders (Hawthorn Leslie 3392 of 1919) which went about its business day after day with no complaint or problems. Nearest the camera is No.22, a former Great Western 0-6-0PT numbered 718. In a previous life it had been Barry Railway 'F' class 0-6-0 tank No.72 which was rebuilt by the GWR. Now, to this writer, this particular pannier tank did not look quite right, either as a pannier on the main line or as an industrial locomotive anywhere. The overhangs seem too long and the wheels look both too small and worn down nearly to the spokes. Perhaps the latter observation is an exaggeration of sorts but the tyres appear extremely thin. No.22 had been withdrawn by the GWR in October 1934 and purchased by ACC during the following January. At the same time ACC also bought GWR No.723, another 0-6-0PT which became No.23. An earlier purchase from the GW, in May 1929, saw a 0-6-0T, No.2161 (ex Brecon & Merthyr No.35), trek to Northumberland to become ACC No.21. *NES 8554.*

As a comparison to No.22 in the previous illustration, we present NCB No.12 which had the same pedigree - Barry Railway F class No.152 - GWR No.747 - built by NBL in 1905, No.16633 - which was purchased by Hartley Main Collieries in September 1932 but not delivered to the company until May 1933 - to become No.25. This 0-6-0 saddletank arrived at Hartley Main with GWR No.724, another 0-6-0ST which became No.24. Our picture shows No.12 at the platform used by miners from the Paddy trains at Weetslade screens, near Burradon, at an unknown date. The engine itself appears to be out of use, as does the colliery which seems rather quiet with not a wagon or soul in sight, whilst the screens are in a state of near dereliction/demolition. Weetslade Colliery closed in 1966 but this view was captured in late 1964. What about those pipes in the foreground which are new and could well be the type used for high pressure water (hydraulics) installations. Have they recently been unloaded from a train or are they awaiting removal to another pit? No.12 was scrapped in April 1965. *NES 8576.*

Bedlington 'A' Colliery in 1970 with NCB outside cylinder 0-6-0ST No.62 (Robert Stephenson & Hawthorn No.7944 of 1957) hauling a loaded six wagon train of internal user wagons away from the screens. No.62 was normally unused during this period but was resurrected annually for a two week spell whilst the diesel shunter was being overhauled. Lifting its first coal in the 1840s, Bedlington became the 'A' pit of the Bedlington group which consisted five different mines at Vesting Day. Located just north of the River Blyth, by the village of Sleekburn, the colliery was connected to the North Eastern's line at Bedlington Junction. Producing in excess of 300,000 tons of saleable coal per annum, Bedlington 'A' employed around 900 men up to closure in 1971. *NES 8656.*

Somewhere on the Backworth system a 21-ton hopper wagon has become derailed bringing operations to a temporary halt in that siding. NCB No.2, a rather smart looking 0-6-0ST is in attendance for a possible pulling out job, achieved with some strategically placed timber, a bit of patience and a bit of know how. The six-coupled tank was another former main line engine purchased from the North Eastern in May 1912 - NER 1350 Class, No.1364 RWH 1671 of 1876 which became Backworth No.7. It was scrapped in April 1954. *NES 8583.*

Although most of the locomotives working on the Backworth system were six-coupled, there were a few four-coupled engines which became NCB property. This is Backworth No.21, a diminutive Manning Wardle 0-4-0ST (MW No.1978 of 1919), posing for the camera on Tuesday 19th June 1951. It was delivered new to the erstwhile East Holywell Coal Co. but ended its days west of Newcastle and was scrapped at West Wylam in June 1961. *NES 8586.*

No.21 lying derelict at West Wylam. Graffiti on the cab side, above the worksplate states - 6-5 Special - which gives us a clue as to the approximate date of the photograph. Pete Murray, Jim Dale, Don Lang & his Frantic Five, etc., were all screened on BBC television from Saturday 16th February 1957 until December 1958, when 'Auntie Beeb' pulled the plug on the show. *NES 8586A.*

Backworth crossing, 1st August 1966. You can tell its August because of the rain. Hudswell Clarke 0-6-0T No.39 (No.1824 of 1949), breasts the road crossing with a loaded train bound for Whitehill Point on the Tyne. During his hours of duty the flagman resided in the crossing cabin on the left, the windows placed so as to give him due warning of an approaching train from either direction. It appears to have been a steady job in its time. Exercise, fresh air, morning papers, novels! The road was the B1322 which, although not readily apparent here, got quite busy sometimes and in June 1969 required both traffic lights and the flagman to control both trains and road traffic. It was not just through trains which passed over the crossing, those shunting the siding on the east side of the line north of the crossing (visible behind the elevated water tank) came back and forth during shunting operations. no doubt it was a popular place with motorists. The Backworth railway system closed in July 1980, shortly after the last of its collieries ceased operation but the Whitehill Point traffic had ceased long before that in 1969. *NES 8589.*

It wasn't just the East Coast Main Line which could boast flat crossings. The Backworth system and the British Railways Blyth & Tyne route also had one on the branch from Backworth to Fenwick Colliery. It was controlled by the BR signal box, Earsdon, seen to the right of the 0-6-0ST 'Austerity' No.33 (RSH 7177 of 1944) which is heading east on its way to Fenwick with a train of empties. *NES 8590.*

Fenwick Colliery, partly visible in the left background, is the location of the sidings being shunted by outside cylinder 0-6-0ST No.24 (HC 1489 of 1922). We have no date for this one but around 1965 should cover it as all of the wagons have the NCB markings, albeit in numerous different styles. Note also that a few steel hopper wagons have crept in amongst the myriad of wooden bodied hoppers. What is remarkable about the trains is the fact that all of the wagons appear to be clean and blemish free! Fenwick closed in 1973. *NES 8590A.*

(*opposite*) **Looking south-east, towards the River Tyne, we are at Percy Main at an unknown date prior to 1953. Getting underway from the sidings with a load of empties, is USA tank No.35 (Davenport 2509 of 1943) which came to Europe in 1944 to join the United States Army Transportation Corps as their No.1944. With the cessation of hostilities and the rebuilding of railway systems on the Continent well under way, this particular 0-6-0T which did not in fact have to leave British shores and was put up for sale. Purchased in May 1947 by the fledgling NCB, it was put to work hauling full trains of coal from Hartley Main and Seaton Delaval collieries to the exchange sidings at Percy Main over what had once been the Seghill Coal Company Waggonway dating from 1840. Primarily intended for shunting duties when built for the USATC, the NCB put No.35 into virtual main-line service on the Percy Main jobs, returning, as here, with empty wagons for the pits. In mileage terms the USA tank certainly clocked them up over the seven years of its employment. Perhaps that was a factor in its early retirement and scrapping in May 1953. Besides this engine and the aforementioned No.36, another USA tank entered NCB service, USATC No.4372 (Davenport 2521 of 1943) went as No.4 in June 1947 to what had previously been the Wallsend & Hebburn Coal Co's Rising Sun Colliery. *NES 8561.***

Tudhoe Coke Ovens, Spennymoor, 27th March 1954. The two locomotives which worked this facility are paraded in the yard on this sunny and unusually warm day in early Spring. The larger of the two, and leading the parade, is No.5 a twice rebuilt 0-6-0ST which started life as a four-coupled saddletank, its builder unknown. Its first recorded rebuilding took place in 1910, carried out by Hawthorn Leslie. This was followed in 1925 by a further rebuilding at Thornley Colliery. By the time of this photograph the engine was 'spare' and spent much of its time in the shed at Tudhoe. Most of the work was performed by our second engine, No.21 an 0-4-0ST built in 1919 by Kerr Stuart (No.4028). Both locomotives were retired in September 1955 when the ovens were shut down. Breaking up of the pair followed in March 1956. *NES 8725A.*

Newfield Colliery & Brickworks, 3rd September 1958. Peckett 0-4-0ST (No.916 of 1901) was numbered 1, although it is not apparent from this view. The colliery here was owned by Dorman Long, that company having acquired it in November 1929 from the Bolckow, Vaughan & Co. In 1927 Newfield mine, which had re-opened in 1921, was connected underground with Byers Green Colliery, about a mile to the east. This increased output slightly and this four-coupled saddletank arrived from West Auckland Colliery. Tucked away on a hillside overlooking the River Wear, Newfield Colliery was connected to the Bishop Auckland-Durham line via a one mile spur from the main line just north of Hunwick passenger station (opened April 1857, closed May 1964). Running north-eastwards past the site of the abandoned Hunwick mine (closed 1921), the spur crossed the Wear before heading into a dead-end shunt on the opposite bank. A reverse was then required along the east bank of the river to set back into the colliery site which had become a drift mine at some time prior to WW2. The output from the mine was enough to feed the brickworks which specialised in firebricks, however, the output of the mine was below the 150 tons a day which would have seen it join the NCB in 1947. Dorman Long, requiring firebricks on a continuing basis for their various iron and steel processes, kept the brickworks going for a number of years after the coal seam had run out in 1959. Although the drift had finished, the brickworks carried on using this 0-4-0ST until road transport took over in 1962. The little Peckett and its then recently arrived newer partner from Dorman Long, another 0-4-0ST No.43, were both abandoned and cut up by the summer. *NES 8730.*

23

The Dorman Long 0-4-0ST No.43 which ended its life at Newfield brickworks along with Peckett No.1. This picture was captured in the 1950s at the Britannia works in Middlesbrough when the 0-4-0ST was working for the steel production side of Dorman Long. Built by the company in 1949, No.43 carries the large distinctive numberplates associated with Dorman Long locomotives. *NES 8715.*

An unusually dirty member of the Dorman Long fleet in March 1952 was No.37, a Barclay 0-4-0ST dating from 1937. Adding to the pollution of the locality, the locomotive was working in the Acklam steel works complex at Middlesbrough. *NES 8718A.*

The most extensive railway system, and with it the largest locomotive fleet, inherited by the National Coal Board in County Durham was that of the Lambton, Hetton & Joicey Collieries Ltd. Most of the mines were situated inland whereas the staiths, which accounted for the Company's sea borne coal trade, were located on the south bank of the River Wear at Sunderland. Furthest away from the river staiths, at nearly ten miles distance, was the Hetton part of the group which though having a direct connection to the river over its own railway, was somewhat restricted by four inclines. The Lambton complex on the other hand, had no direct connection and instead used running powers over the North Eastern Railway's Leamside to Sunderland route to gain access to the river staiths and to its satellite installations on the north bank of the Wear at Harraton Colliery and a chemical works at Washington. This view shows one of the distinctive 0-6-2 tank engines, No.42 (Robert Stephenson No.3801 of 1920), running over NCB metals at New Penshaw with a train of empties bound for Lambton Colliery on 4th September 1956. The British Railway tracks ran through the wider span of the bridge in the background whilst the NCB trackage was bridged by the shorter span. No.42 lasted in service until February 1969 when it was condemned. It was cut up at Philadelphia in May 1970 by a scrap merchant from Gateshead. *NES 8621.*

On a warm Monday, 8th September 1952, 0-6-2T No.10 (Robert Stephenson No.3378 of 1909), negotiates BR metals at Fawcett Street Junction with a heavy load of coal for the staiths at Sunderland South Dock. The line branching off to the north, just visible above the locomotive, led to Sunderland station. *NES 8621.*

A closer look at No.10 outside the engine shed at Philadelphia during its NCB career. Although not immaculately turned out and having suffered a long gouge on the side tank, the 0-6-2T still looked respectable sporting full lining and a works plate with picked-out lettering. It was whilst undergoing a scheduled overhaul in October 1965, that the engine was withdrawn from service after the repairs were cancelled! Languishing on site at Philadelphia until January 1969 it was eventually cut up there. To the left of the shed is the ramped line leading to the elevated coaling stage which will be illustrated later. *NES 8631.*

Lambton staiths, Sunderland, on the last day of May 1955 with 0-4-0 saddletank LH&JC No.17 (Manning Wardle No.2023 of 1923) hauling empty hopper wagons off No.10 staith back to the departure sidings. So extensive were the staiths here - covering nearly a thousand yards of river frontage and actually split into two separate sites Lambton and Hetton - that the LH&JC Co. built an engine shed at the former place to house the eight or so 0-4-0 tank engines employed specifically at the staiths. No.17 was not a permanent resident of this particular site and was allocated at various times to either the Lambton staiths, Hetton colliery or to Philadelphia from where it was sent to different parts of the inland railway network. As the collieries of its parent system became exhausted and coal discharge into sea going vessels on the River Wear lessened (although more than half a million tons were discharged into ships holds here in 1960), it became more difficult to justify using the saddletank and it was laid up at Philadelphia during 1960 and eventually scrapped in August of that year. Of the two groups of staiths, the Hetton lot closed in 1962 whereas the Lambton group survived until the first week of 1967 when they too were shut down having fallen into disuse some months previously. The area immediately beneath the photographer was called Galley's Gill and the corrugated roof of the engine shed can be seen at right. Such was the height of the staiths above the river that colliers moored alongside could be hidden from anyone working in this yard, or indeed from those at this elevated position. *NES 8627.*

Outside the engine shed at Lambton staiths, NCB No.38 basks in the midday sun circa summer 1960. One of the more modern steam locomotives employed at this location, the 0-4-0ST was built for the NCB in 1953 by Robert Stephenson & Hawthorn (Works No.7756) and was one of a pair [NCB No.39, RSH 7757 of 1953] bought to work the staiths here. No.38 moved away from the old LH&JC system in July 1965 and was sent to Seaham Colliery on the coast. Being surplus to requirements by now, No.38 was condemned and sold for scrap in March 1968 but the original scrap metal dealer sold on the 0-4-0ST to Willoughby's who operated at Ashington; they took the engine back to Northumberland in September 1968 and it was cut up soon afterwards. Sister No.39 continued working at Lambton staiths until they closed in January 1967. Afterwards it moved across the river to Wearmouth Colliery and further employment but moved on eighteen months later to Hylton Colliery at Castletown just west of Wearmouth and on the north bank of the Wear. Another locomotive surplus to requirements, No.39 was scrapped on site at Hylton in December 1972. *NES 8785.*

Back at Philadelphia, the elevated coaling stage forms an interesting backdrop to a busy scene in the engine yard during the early NCB years. Stealing the daylight from an unidentified Austerity tank and 0-6-2T No.5, is No.1 - the oldest resident of the Lambton system in NCB days - built by Hudswell & Clarke in 1866, their 71st locomotive. Note it has a deep bufferbeam which enabled it to propel narrow bodied, dumb buffered wagons such as the chaldrons, although there seems little evidence that the engine has used that facility of late. The inside cylinder 0-6-0, which had undergone numerous changes over its lifetime, was scrapped in August 1954. Over the coaling stage storage hoppers are two coal wagons one of which is still lettered LHJC. *NES 8633.*

The larger of the locomotive running sheds at Philadelphia is illustrated here with Hudswell Clarke built, No.230 of 1881, LH&JC 0-4-0ST No.22 taking centre stage on 16th October 1953. Sold for scrap in January 1957, the engine apparently lingered at Philadelphia until broken up some eighteen months later. I wonder what happened to the wonderful numberplates? Standing in the left background, Dorothea Colliery which employed just over 600 men at this time, was producing approximately 180 to 200 thousand tons of saleable coal a year. In December 1956 Dorothea was merged with nearby Herrington which was located about a mile to the north. The merger, which more than doubled Herrington's annual output to over half a million tons a year, ensured the latter pit's future until 1985 when the coal industry in Durham virtually collapsed. Dorothea had wound its first coal in 1816, just eleven years after the Battle of Trafalgar, four years after Napoleon's retreat from Moscow and a year after Waterloo whilst steam railways were a thing of the future. *NES 8641*.

It is August 1962 and another of the former LH&JC 0-6-2T fleet, No.31 (Kitson 4533/07), stands in the locomotive servicing area alongside the coaling stage at Philadelphia shed. By now the cleaning standards of NCB locomotives have started to slip and a general feel of neglect is beginning to creep in, noticed more perhaps by outsiders rather than those working in the coal industry. Dorothea's headframe still stands, although the ground buildings have long gone, whilst the shaft itself was retained for ventilation and for an emergency exit from the Herrington underground complex. *NES 9747.*

Former LH&J 0-6-0ST No.45 (HL No.2932 of 1912) wearing the colours of the NCB - somewhere under the grime - stands beneath the coaling gantry at Philadelphia on 22nd August 1968. This locomotive joined the Durham system in 1923 from Silksworth Colliery. It first glance this could be an Austerity which has been through the Lambton works for a cab job but that is not the case. The end of steam on the Lambton system is but six months away, and the BR D95XX diesel-hydraulics are massing at various BR locations along with numerous 0-6-0 diesel-electric shunters - one of the D95XX locomotives is apparently already at Lambton works having arrived from Wearmouth Colliery. Our No.45 here was one of the casualties of the February 1969 changeover but it hung around until December 1970 before it was cut-up on site. *NES 9740.*

On that same day in August 1968 another of the Lambton system saddletanks came alongside the coaling gantry. This time it was outside cylinder No.63, one of the larger 0-6-0s supplied by Robert Stephenson & Hawthorn in 1949 (No.7600). No.63 had reallocated from South Hetton Railways in November 1958. It too was scrapped on site, somewhat earlier, in May 1970. *NES 9774*.

Back in the days when the National Coal Board was still a young organisation with big ideas and deep pockets, the locomotive fleet at some locations took on the new identity in varying shades of green, blue, black and red. In June 1951 this is how Robert Stephenson & Co. supplied this 0-6-0 No.20 appeared outside the shed at Philadelphia, green fresh and not quite looking its age of 75 years (RS 2260 of 1876). Incredibly, No.20 worked for another nine years or so before becoming uneconomical to repair. It was scrapped in the summer of 1960. *NES 9887.*

Staying on the South Hetton Coal Co. system but going back in time to circa 1947, we move south to South Hetton Railway where this 0-4-0 saddletank awaits its fate. No.19 in the LH&JC fleet, the little outside cylinder locomotive was one Manning Wardle's products, No.344 of 1871. It had seem better days and although taken over by the NCB in January 1947, it was laid up by November of the same year. Close inspection of the base of the chimney will reveal numerous holes which would have been difficult to patch and new chimneys of that profile would have been difficult to come by. The spectacle glasses in the cab have also been broken, the bufferbeam is bent and further corrosion around the base of the bunker and over the firebox cover has rendered this engine unserviceable. Broken up in August 1954, there would not be much, if anything, worth salvaging from this one. *NES 8637.*

Former London & North Eastern Railway Y7 class 0-4-0T No.898 was built by the North Eastern Railway at its Gateshead works in December 1888. In April 1929 it was sold for £250 to Ord & Maddison Ltd. for use at their Crossthwaite whinstone quarry in Middleton-in-Teesdale. Another Y7 (LNER No.1302, Gateshead, September 1891) was purchased by Ord & Maddison in March 1930 for the same price. It too was put to work at the Crossthwaite site. Both locomotives continued in employment at the site, hauling stone from the quarry to the railhead with the LNER. Road transport took over the transportation of the quarry products and the rail system was abandoned. However, both of the Y7s were used by scrap metal contractors Arnott, Young & Co. to help in the dismantling of the railway facilities at the quarries in 1952. Still in relatively good condition, No.898 is dumped, awaiting cutting up, at Middleton-in-Teesdale in September 1952. No.1302 had apparently been dealt with by Arnott Young a few days earlier. *NES 8700A.*

The engine shed at Doxford's, Sunderland in the early Fifties' with four of the crane tanks and a solitary saddletank on view. The saddletank - the second to carry the name GENERAL for the company - appears to be the younger of the two, a Peckett 0-4-0ST (No.2049 of 1944), acquired third-hand in April 1951. The original GENERAL, another 0-4-0 Peckett engine (No.703 from 1899) was scrapped in May 1951. All the engines here carried names but during WW2 two Hawthorn Leslie 0-4-0ST worked the shipyard and they were numbered 2 and 33, however, they were both on loan from coal concerns and returned to their owners around 1945. The shed roof, or at least its corrugated cladding, was to disappear in latter years. *NES 8687.*

A close-up of two of the crane tanks, both unidentified but both having different lining on the front faces of their side tanks. This scene was captured at about the same time as the previous illustration. It gives a good idea of the location of the engine shed perched as it was on the steep slope of the south bank of the River Wear. The Queen Alexandra bridge, which spanned not just the river but the shipyard too, dominates the background. The lateness of the hour can be appreciated by the shadows, so the three gentlemen approaching the camera must have just finished work for the day. *NES 8687A.*

Not all of the Doxford locomotive fleet could stable within the engine shed so a couple of the arches carrying the Queen Alexandra bridge were utilised for stabling. This is WEAR, a rebuilt former 0-4-0 crane tank originally supplied by Hawthorn Leslie (No.2551 of 1903). Looking very smart, this undated picture of the 0-4-0T shows off the massive bufferbeams which were a load on their own. Besides this engine, there was another HL crane tank from the same era - DEPTFORD, No.2535 of 1902 - which had also been rebuilt in having the crane removed. It was scrapped in April 1949 whereas the subject of this picture lasted until September 1952. Note that the arch immediately behind WEAR has the remains of a wooden screen and doorway still attached to the stonework - are those the discarded doors propped against the wall behind the engineman? *NES 8686.*

41

Randolph Colliery and its adjacent coking plant, at Evenwood, was perched on a tract of high ground approximately two miles west of West Auckland. The nearest railway, the Bishop Auckland-Barnard Castle line and an adjoining freight branch to Butterknowle, was just under a mile away to the north, winding through the valley of the River Gaunless. However, the colliery was some 150 or so higher than the railway which required the building of a self-acting 1260 yard long incline to join the two. This is the top of the incline in May 1954 with the colliery headframe just visible through the arch of the incline drum house, the rest of the installation is the coking plant. Randolph Colliery started winding coal in 1895 and employed over 400 men producing more than 100,000 tons annually. Much of the production went next door to the coking plant which was a separate enterprise from the mining operation. It was the coke which became the main product descending the incline with four loaded 21-ton wagons normally descending whilst seven empty hoppers ascended. Note the three running rails employed instead of four rails spread over two separate tracks. The common centre rail, though keeping costs lower, necessitated a passing place at the half way point to allow the groups of wagons to pass each other. At both the top and bottom of the incline the 'twin' rails parted momentarily so that they could then become one track again. This views provides us with a look at the 'parting and joining' of the lines just in front of the drum house - modellers take note of the fixed point of the parting. The two steel ropes, which have scoured the ground and sleepers over the years, are easily discernible, one in the four-foot on the right, the other, complete with its hook, is on the ground in the six-foot between the left rail of the incline and the track holding loaded wagons. The colliery ceased production in 1962 but had in fact been turning out less coal each year from about 1957 onwards so that before the decade was over it became necessary for the coking plant to start importing coal from elsewhere. The self-acting incline then required some assistance so a 70 horsepower motor was installed to haul loaded coal wagons (two at a time) up the slope whilst four hoppers loaded with coke descended. On the left is the siding for full coal wagons which had just been hoisted up and which had left the incline trackage about 100 yards behind the photographer. A 'mirrored' situation existed on the right side of the layout here. Prior to descending the bank, wagons full of coke would be positioned by one of the three steam locomotives employed here. With brakes firmly applied on the wagons, the rope would be attached, the locomotive draw away, brakes off and the wagons would start their descent. A similar operation would have taken place at the foot of the incline to equalise the loading. The coking plant and the incline, all of which had been under private ownership since 1957, ceased operation in 1984. *NES 8734.*

0-4-0ST RANDOLPH dated from 1942 (RSH 7043) and was one of four locomotives which worked the colliery and the coking plant. From May 1957 the coking plant was taken over by a private concern, part of the purchase also included the branch, incline and two locomotives, 0-4-0ST WINSTON (RSH 7159 of 1945) being the other. Both were worked the colliery and coking plant but the former closed in February 1962. Thereafter both engines carried on work at the coking plant delivering and taking wagons from the incline. The coking plant did not close down until May 1984 but the two saddletanks had been retired in early 1969 and later sold for scrap. *NES 8733.*

A 1939 photograph of Manning Wardle 0-4-0ST (No.813 of 1881) at Parsons Byers quarry near Stanhope, County Durham. The little saddletank was numbered 235 in the Dorman Long fleet but it was also named WASP though evidence of the nameplate, or indeed a works plate, seem somewhat lacking. However, the former was possibly painted on in Scottish style and had been lost to years of exposure, cleaning and pollution! This engine had arrived at this Wearside quarry, prior to January 1928, from dealers J.F.Wake & Co., who had in turn got it from Lucas & Aird, the contractors responsible for much of the Hull & Barnsley Railway construction. WASP had apparently taken part in that contract and was used at the quarry here to remove trains of overburden. It was scrapped circa 1943, its remains no doubt helping the war effort. *NES 8669.*

The works shunter at the Forth Bank Works of Robert Stephenson & Hawthorns, Ltd., Newcastle upon Tyne, was this 0-4-0CT built in 1925 (No.3583), during the period when the company was known as R.&W. Hawthorn, Leslie & Co. Ltd. The company built dozens of these crane tanks, chiefly for the numerous shipyards located in the north-east, and elsewhere; the Doxford fleet at Sunderland were all supplied by this company. *NES 8661.*

A rather colourful, gaudy even, but nevertheless nicely turned out pannier tank in industrial service circa 1935. This is former Great Western No.719 which was purchased by the Wallsend & Hebburn Coal Co. in September 1934 to work at Rising Sun Colliery, Wallsend. The 0-6-0PT was built by Sharp Stewart, at their Atlas works in Glasgow (No.4595 of 1900) for the Barry Railway, becoming their No.99. Note the removal (by cold chisel?) of the 7 and 9 on the numberplate. *NES 8662.*

(*opposite*) At the other end of the livery scale we have this specimen which worked the jetty below the cliffs on which Skinningrove Iron Works were located. The 0-4-0 would not look out of place on a film set with gun barrels poking out of its various orifices. Beneath the plated exterior skin was a vertical boilered tank engine, built in 1871 by Cochranes of Middlesbrough. When the 'armour plating' was fitted is unknown but in September 1952 it was beginning to show signs of deterioration on account of the sea water which continually splashed over it during choppy weather. Note the sand covering everything within reach of the waves, helped no doubt by the near continual winds. Working this jetty certainly had its drawbacks and would require a certain amount of dedication by enginemen. There again there must have been some perks in the summer! But it was a long winter at Skinningrove. *NES 9853.*

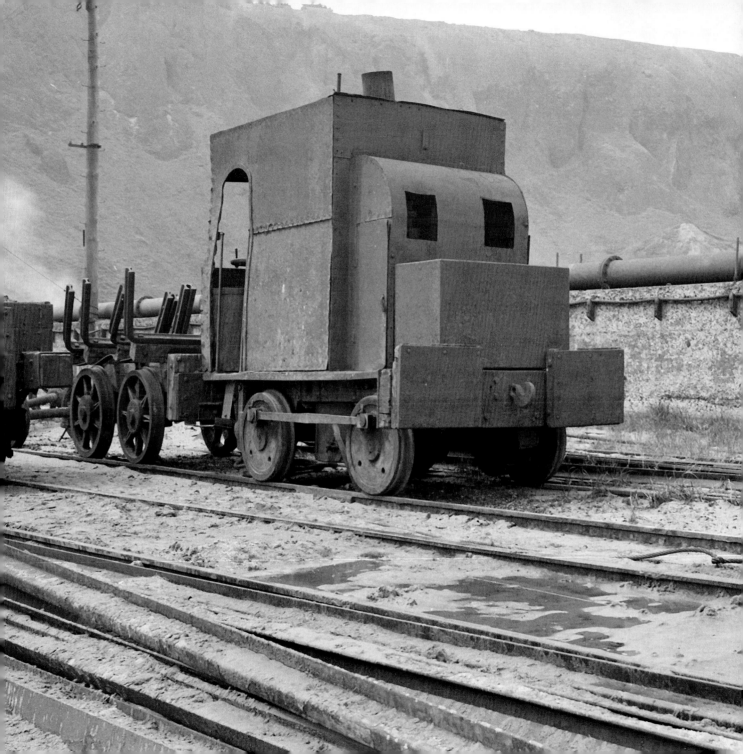

Carville power station, Wallsend, Newcastle, 1st September 1959. This is CEGB No.11 (Hawthorn Leslie No.3641 of 1926), a rather attractive 0-4-0ST which arrived at this power plant in 1936 from Dunston 'A' power station. Both plants were then part of the North-Eastern Electric Supply Co. Ltd. and required a sizeable fleet of locomotives, including electric and diesel types. By now part of the CEGB empire, No.11 left Carville in November 1960 to work at Darlington power station. It was scrapped in 1969. *NES 8776.*

Seemingly out of reach from the ground, CEGB 4w electric locomotives Nos.2 and 1 go about their business whilst traversing this lofty structure past the cabs of shipyard cranes and over the rooftops of industrial Wallsend at Carville power station in 1963. Locomotive No.2 was a British Thompson-Houston product of 1901 vintage whilst No.1 was built in the United States by Baldwin Locomotive Works, Philadelphia in 1903, works No.21749. Similar locomotives worked at other Newcastle power stations and at one in Sunderland. *NES 8778.*

No.1 TEAM VALLEY ESTATE is the legend carried by this Hawthorn Leslie 0-6-0ST - No.3934 of 1937 - which was the first locomotive acquired by the newly developed company which ran the trading estate situated on the west side of the East Coast Main Line, just south of the Tyne, at Low Fell in September 1937. The saddletank was actually delivered in January 1938 by Robert Stephenson & Hawthorn the compant created by the merger of HL with Robert Stephenson. This 1963 view shows the engine in the livery it carried throughout its life. On the top of the smokebox door a TV monogram, with the stem of the T inside the V, was fitted; a similar monogram adorned the rear of the coal bunker. Working alone until 1949, No.1 was then joined by a Peckett 0-4-0ST (No.2042 of 1943) which was numbered 8 and was formerly employed on the ex Royal Ordnance site which became Aycliffe Trading Estate. That was another site owned and run by North Eastern Trading Estates, the owners of TVTE. No.1 was scrapped in 1965, its stablemate No.8 having succumbed in the January of the previous year. Both engines were superseded by another older Peckett saddletank, ROF 0-4-0 No.7 (P No.2016 of 1941) which arrived at Team Valley in August 1963, also from the Aycliffe site. *NES 8779.*

Here is that last member of the Team Valley Trading Estate locomotive fleet, Peckett 2016 carrying the nameplate ROF 9 No.7 from its war years at Aycliffe. Much of the 700 acre Team Valley site was pleasantly open, as shown by this view of No.7 in 1963, but industry was always within sight, and smelling distance, with Norwood coking plant at the north end of the railway and collieries all around. This 0-4-0ST was hired out to the NCB during 1964-66 and worked at Pelaw Main on the Bowes Railway. It was scrapped in the summer of 1966. *NES 8780*.

Dent's Wharf, Middlesbrough Docks, Wednesday, 20th June 1951. Taking centre stage is T.Roddam Dent No.2, a Chapman & Furneaux 0-4-0ST (No.1212 of 1901). It must be lunchtime or a teabreak as the engine is left to its own devices with not a soul in sight. Amid the scrap, railway wagons, various sheds, warehouses and general clutter found around dock installations during that period, are a few unfamiliar and perhaps 'out of place' items. Note the little Austin motor car, registration BRM682, with its AA badge attached to the front of the radiator just like a shedplate - was that the photographer's own vehicle? Admitted the radiator grill was the obvious place to fix the badge without resorting to a special bracket. And what was that 'Chivers Jellies' van doing there? *NES 9846.*

HAZELS was the name carried by this Chapman & Furneaux 0-4-0 well tank seen in a derelict condition at its former place of work in Aycliffe quarry on 23rd June 1951. This locomotive was apparently the only standard gauge well tank constructed by its makers and was built in 1900 (works No.1189) for the St Helens glass manufacturers Pilkington Brothers. By 1923 the Lancashire company had finished with the services of the 0-4-0WT and it was put up for sale. By June 1923 the owners of the Aycliffe quarry, Aycliffe Lime & Limestone Co. Ltd, had purchased the engine for use at the quarry sidings, situated on the west side of the ECML just north of Darlington, immediately south of Aycliffe passenger station. The sidings had previously been shunted with engines supplied by agreement from the North Eastern Railway. (*inset*) The works plate carried by HAZELS even during its period of dereliction at the Aycliffe quarry. The locomotive was scrapped in 1951 (whatever happened to those name and works plates?) at an unknown location but possibly at Hanratty's scrap yard near North Road station in Darlington. *NES 9843 & 9843A.*

Now for a look at some narrow gauge specimens - 2ft 0in. to be exact - at Barrasford quarry in the north Tyne valley in April 1953. This is No.4, a 4-wheel Sentinel (No.5989 of 1925) without any wheels at this time but waiting patiently for their return. The railway system at this place ceased to operate and closed in June 1958 but it nevertheless added to the myriad of narrow gauge railways which served the industry of Great Britain during the Twentieth century. *NES 8655.*

Barrasford quarry No.3, also pictured in April 1953, looking the worse for wear on the day but nevertheless working merrily, the 4-wheel locomotive hauls (guides more like) a sizeable train of eleven hoppers, containing Northumberland Whinstone, down the valley. The profile of the smoke coming from the stack would suggest a fair turn of speed but wind on these high slopes is probably more the case. No.3 was another Sentinel machine - note the likeness to No.4 - works number 5990 also of 1925. *NES 8654A.*

Back to standard gauge. In 1941 the Consett Iron Works took delivery of a newly built long-boilered 0-6-0PT (RSH No.7029) which was numbered A19, denoting 'A' class No.19 in the company fleet. A19 was in fact the last of her kind, built to a design first produced in 1872 and popular amongst the various industries of the north-east, especially the Consett Ironmasters. Indeed A19 did not arrive at Consett on her own; two other locomotives of the same type from the same makers (RSH Nos.7027 and 7028) were built with her. They were numbered A1 and A2 in the company scheme but only A1 went to Consett, A2 was allocated to Derwenthaugh Coke Ovens, another arm of the vast Consett empire. Here is A19 outside the Templetown engine shed in Consett at an unknown date, but certainly late Fifties, in the company of an unidentified B class 0-4-0ST and a Hunslet diesel mechanical locomotive which was also camera shy. During the scheme to completely dieselise the company fleet, A19 was sold for scrap in March 1962. However, one of the Consett fleet, A5 of 1883, was preserved. *NES 8648.*

The Consett Iron Works in County Durham had a vast fleet of locomotives amongst them over twenty crane tanks of different types. One of the more conventional examples was this Andrew Barclay 0-4-0CT (No.1715), delivered new in 1920, and numbered D17 in their fleet. The exact date of the photograph is unknown but the two Brush Bagnall Traction diesel electrics in the background, Consett fleet Nos.5 and 6, were delivered new in 1951 (works Nos.3020 and 3021). The crane tank was scrapped in February 1955. Meanwhile, the two diesels proved to be the only ones of their ilk to join the Consett fleet, the company preferring the Hunslet 0-6-0 diesel mechanical which started to appear from 1947 onwards, later followed by 0-4-0DM and 0-6-0 diesel hydraulics in 1959. *NES 8645.*

Want something heavy lifting and shifting? Send for these lads. The ultimate in rail-bourne, compact, mobile cranes. 2-4-0CT E No.1 was a Black Hawthorn machine purchased by the Consett Iron Co. in 1887 (No.897). The design was a collaboration between the makers and the Consett Chief Engineer a Mr.J.P.Roe. Able to lift twelve tons against the normal four tons offered by other crane tanks, this machine was extremely useful and in much demand throughout the site. It appears somewhat complicated but no doubt it was soon mastered by enginemen and fitters alike. Two of the design were in fact built, the twin being E No.2 (BH898 of 1887). The latter crane lasted until August 1955 when it was condemned but it held on at Consett providing spares for E No.1 until February 1964 when it was cut up. Want to see E No.1 today? Try Beamish museum because it was donated to them in 1978. *NES 8646.*

NCB No.48 passed to the nationalised concern from Consett Iron Co. as A No.14, via the Chopwell & Garsfield Railway on 1st January 1947. Built by Hawthorn Leslie in 1914 (No.3080). In October 1960 it moved on to Derwenthaugh Railways. Here, alongside the Derwenthaugh engine shed at Swalwell it looks resplendent in its NCB livery. The 0-6-0PT was scrapped on site in June 1964. *NES 8647.*

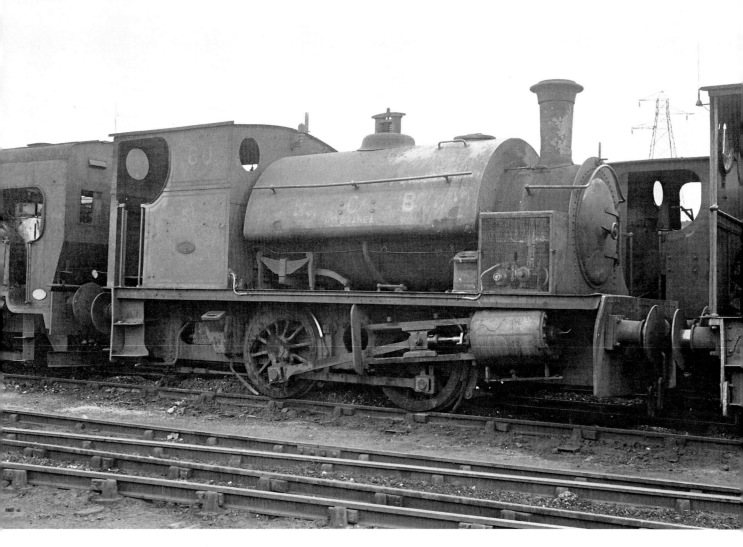

August 1962 and locomotives are gathered together for the weekend at Derwenthaugh shed yard. Amongst the throng of tank engines large and small, clean and dirty, orthodox and unorthodox is NCB No.60, which had started life as a Hawthorn Leslie 0-4-0ST (No.3752 of 1930) but had been rebuilt by the NCB at the Derwenthaugh works in 1961. A regular on the Chopwell & Garsfield Railway, the saddletank was out of use by October 1960 with a poorly boiler hence the 'rebuilding' which, except for that boiler change, very little is known although the caged pumps above the cylinder may have had something to do with it. *NES 9743.*

Derwenthaugh engine shed showing the stabled locomotives during another quiet weekend in August 1962. Identifiable on the shed road is an 'A' class 0-6-0PT. The others are saddletanks, the one at centre looking suspiciously like No.60 with the caged pumps on the right running plate. *NES 8601.*

Although A No.13 was apparently off the property and allocated to what was to become NCB Durham No.6 Area at Vesting Day, by June 1951 it was back at Consett working within the steel works complex, although shedded at the new Leadgate shed, looking none the worse for the experience except perhaps being a bit more grimy. Standing on the threshold of the running shed, it has another, albeit unidentified member of the class behind it. This engine was the only one of its type to be built in Whitehaven, Cumberland. New Lowca Engineering were responsible for its construction, working to the drawings supplied by the CIC. *NES 9885*.

A No.4 was one of the younger members of the class resident at Consett, its makers number being 3952 of 1938. Shortly before this picture was captured, No.4 was converted to oil burning but that was short-lived and it was removed only to be refitted and finally removed again in April 1953. The large container on the cab roof must have been the oil reservoir. In November 1957 the 0-6-0PT went off to work for the NCB from Leadgate engine shed where it was renumbered 91 although there appears to have been some type of arrangement going on between the CIC and the NCB because, after retirement, No.4 was returned to the CIC for scrapping in February 1964. *NES 9886.*

The legend above the worksplate on the cabside of the 0-6-0ST states HARTON UNIT which encompassed a number of the north-east Durham collieries - Boldon, Harton, Westoe and Whitburn - and their associated railway systems. The picture is taken at Boldon Colliery in the mid-fifties when the Hudswell Clarke (1513 of 1924) built engine was working the screens. Although here the engine is carrying no identity except NCB and the aforementioned colliery name, it did, apparently, towards the end of its life carry the name BOLDON No.1513. It is, again, unknown if this consisted a cast plate or simply a painted insignia. The engine was scrapped in December 1959. *NES 9890.*

The South Shields, Marsden & Whitburn Colliery Railway was another passenger carrying colliery concern inherited by the NCB although this one had no physical connection to the main line railway system. Here near Marsden at an unknown date circa 1953, NCB No.6, one of the Westinghouse fitted members of the SSM&WCR fleet (RSH 7603 of 1949), heads towards South Shields (Westoe Lane) with a six vehicle train of ancient six-wheel carriages. The carriage stock on the railway was made up of a mixture of Great North of Scotland Railway vintage and latterly North Sunderland Railway coaches. Opened in 1888 to carry coal from Whitburn Colliery to Harton staiths, it was known locally as the 'Marsden Rattler' and had been granted a Light Railway Order in 1926 to enable it to carry not just miners to and from their work but also members of the public, something it had been doing since opening day anyway. Three stations were located along its length, Westoe Lane at the northern extremity, Marsden Cottage as the intermediate station but which was nothing more than a halt, and the terminus at Whitburn Colliery. Even towards the end of its life, the railway operated twelve trains on weekdays around the clock albeit near to the colliery shift changing periods. The motive power prior to 1949 comprised three Westinghouse fitted 0-6-0 tender engines, with origins back to the 1880s although the oldest of them, No.5, which was built by the North Eastern Railway at Gateshead in 1881, was the last of the trio to be retired in 1952. The three replacements, all RSH outside cylinder, 0-6-0ST which arrived between 1949 and 1952, were likewise fitted with the Westinghouse equipment. However, their reign on the passenger trains was somewhat short as the service was withdrawn in late November 1953. The Westinghouse pumps and associated air storage tank are easily spotted on No.6. *NES 8603.*

Two of the SSM&WCR passenger vehicles laid up after their November 1953 retirement. The external condition of the nearest six-wheeler is rather rough but for how long it had been on this siding, along with its exact vintage is unknown (probably one of the ex GNSR set bought in 1938). *NES 8605.*

Springwell Bank Foot locomotive shed on the Bowes Railway, near Wardley. This small shed was situated, as the name implies, at the foot of the Springwell incline (immediately behind the camera), on the east side of the line. We are looking north-east here, towards Jarrow staiths approximately four miles distant. The original two-road running shed was constructed in stone and dated from the 1850s. More than likely, the original entrances would have been arched but lintels took their place when the openings were made wider to accommodate larger locomotives. The one-road brick extension on the west wall was from a much later date and was used as a repair shop complete with outside shearlegs. One of its former occupants, alas unidentified stables outside in the stub siding minus its boiler. Outside the repair shop a saddletank waits patiently at the door whilst to its left is No.23 a rebuilt 0-6-0ST which was cut up at this shed by an outside contractor in January 1971. The running shed was also used for repairs and the last locomotive to get any attention there was Austerity 0-6-0ST No.90 in October 1965. *NES 8607.*

Seaham Harbour Dock Co. 0-6-0ST SEAHAM, a Peckett engine (No.1052), was purchased new in 1905 for the opening of the new South Dock at Seaham in the November of that year. Three coal berths, able to accommodate the largest colliers of the time could be loaded at the same time. This 0-6-0ST, together with an eclectic mix of other locomotives, of varying pedigree and ability, handled the wagons on and off the staiths. In 1906 another similar Peckett engine (No.1083) carrying the name of SILKSWORTH and only the second new locomotive bought in, joined the fleet. The large buffer blocks fixed to SEAHAM gives an idea of the types of wagons it was shunting about the place. By 1961 younger second-hand locomotives took over the shunting of the staiths and our 0-6-0ST was withdrawn and scrapped. Its sister engine of 1906 lasted until July 1963. *NES 8614.*

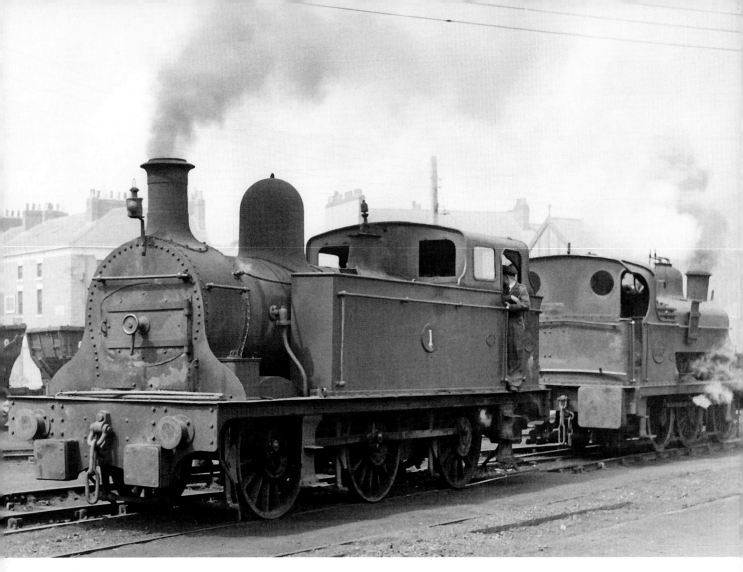

Polluting the locality with impunity, SHDC 0-6-0T No.1 SEATON in the company of another offender, in the shape of 0-6-0ST MARS, add to the ambience of what was Seaham. No.1 was built by the Londonderry Railway in 1902 but apparently not put into service until January 1906 and then it went straight to the Dock Co. MARS was much older (RS 2238 of 1875) and was built for the North Eastern Railway as a '964' class, its final number, before joining the SHDC in December 1908, being 1661. SEATON was taken out of service and scrapped in May 1962 whilst MARS was broken up the following year. *NES 8615A.*

Almost dwarfed by the 21-ton hopper wagons behind it, SHDC No.18 (Lewin No.683 of 1877) had been built as an 0-4-0WT but was later (circa 1899) rebuilt at Seaham in this guise. It is now preserved at Beamish, looking slightly better than it did here on 22nd August 1968. *NES 8618A.*

Ex Consett 0-4-0ST B No.16 arrived at East Hedley Hope Colliery on loan from Langley Park Colliery in March 1950. The reason for its arrival at EHHC was to help with shunting as the colliery's own locomotive, also numbered 16 (Robert Stephenson No.2325 of 1894) was broken down and required major workshop repairs. Up to B No.16 coming onto the property, the colliery had to rely on road tractors to push and pull the wagons around the site. Even though production was only about 100,000 tons a year, that still equated to two thousand tons a week that had to be shifted off the site. The former Consett Iron Works saddletank was also a Robert Stephenson product, No.2725 of 1890, which had been with the Consett company from new but at Vesting Day was actually located at Langley Park Colliery so became part of the NCB fleet, albeit never losing its former identity. It returned to Langley Park during the summer of 1950 and worked there for another eleven years before being scrapped in February 1962. *NES 9893.*

The Dorman Long ship loading facility at Port Clarence on the north bank of the River Tees, opposite Middlesbrough docks, required the employment of this Black Hawthorn 0-4-0ST (No.973 of 1889) in June 1951. The tank was numbered 5 in the Dorman Long fleet but note that the numberplate is nothing like the exuberant examples adorning the engines employed within the various steel producing plants. This installation was built on land which had been reclaimed from the sea, a process that went on for decades in this corner of County Durham. *NES 9898.*